Fiddle Time Runners

T0087027

Violin accompaniment book

Kathy and David Blackwell

Teacher's note

These duet parts are written to accompany the tunes in *Fiddle Time Runners*. They are an alternative to the piano accompaniments or audio tracks, and are not designed to be used with those items. These parts may be used with violins playing together with violas (using *Viola Time Runners* and playing the ensemble parts where appropriate); a separate viola duet book is available providing duet parts for all the additional tunes in *Viola Time Runners*.

We are grateful to Simon Stace for all his help in road-testing these duets.

Kathy and David Blackwell

OXFORD
UNIVERSITY PRESS

OXFORD
UNIVERSITY PRESS

Great Clarendon Street, Oxford OX2 6DP,
United Kingdom

Oxford University Press is a department of the University of Oxford.
It furthers the University's objective of excellence in research, scholarship,
and education by publishing worldwide. Oxford is a registered trade mark of
Oxford University Press in the UK and in certain other countries

This collection © Oxford University Press 1998, 2003, 2005, 2013, and 2023

Unless marked otherwise, all pieces are by Kathy and David Blackwell and are
© Oxford University Press. All traditional and composed pieces are
arranged by Kathy and David Blackwell and are © Oxford University Press.
Unauthorized arrangement or photocopying of this copyright material is ILLEGAL.

Kathy and David Blackwell have asserted their right under the Copyright,
Designs and Patents Act, 1988, to be identified as the Composers of this Work.

Database right Oxford University Press (maker)

Impression: 1

All rights reserved. No part of this publication may be reproduced,
stored in a retrieval system, or transmitted, in any form or by any means,
without the prior permission in writing of Oxford University Press

Permission to perform the works in this anthology in public
(except in the course of divine worship) should normally be obtained from
a local performing right licensing organization, unless the owner or the occupier
of the premises being used already holds a licence from such an organization.
Likewise, permission to make and exploit a recording of these works
should be obtained from a local mechanical copyright licensing organization

Enquiries concerning reproduction outside the scope of the above
should be directed to the Music Rights Department, Oxford University Press, at
music.permissions.uk@oup.com or at the address above

ISBN: 978-0-19-356616-3

Cover illustration by Martin Remphry

Music and text origination by Katie Johnston and Julia Bovee
Printed in Great Britain

Contents

1. Start the show 4
2. Banyan tree 5
3. Heat haze 6
4. Medieval tale 7
5. Cornish May song 8
6. Chase in the dark 9
7. Merrily danced the Quaker's wife 10
8. O leave your sheep 11
9. Jazzy Jingle bells (J. Pierpont) 12
10. Allegretto in G (Mozart) 13
11. The Mallow fling 14
12. Noël (Daquin) 15
13. Finale from the 'Water Music' (Handel) 16
14. Ecossaise in G (Beethoven) 17
15. Fiddle Time rag 18
16. Busy day 20
17. On the go! 21
18. Yodelling song 22
19. Takin' it easy 24
20. Romani band 23
21. Ten thousand miles away 28
22. I got those fiddle blues 26
23. Air in G (J. C. Bach) 27
24. Prelude from 'Te Deum' (Charpentier) 29
25. That's how it goes! 30
26. Hari coo coo 31
27. Summer evening 32
28. Flamenco dance 32
29. Adam in the garden 34
30. Somebody's knocking at your door 36
31. The old chariot 37
32. Air (Handel) 38
33. The wee cooper o' Fife 39
34. Winter song 40
35. Rory O'More 41
36. Trick cyclist 42
37. Aerobics! 43
38. Caribbean sunshine 44

1. Start the show

KB & DB

24
f
f
2. Banyan tree
Jamaican folk tune
Gently
mf
mf
cresc.
cresc.
mf
mf
6
mp
mp
11
mf
mf
16
mp
mp
rit.

3. Heat haze

KB & DB

4. Medieval tale

KB & DB

5. Cornish May song

Cornish folk tune

6. Chase in the dark

KB & DB

7. Merrily danced the Quaker's wife

Scottish folk tune

8. O leave your sheep

9. Jazzy Jingle bells

J. Pierpont

10. Allegretto in G

11. The Mallow fling

Irish folk tune

12. Noël

Daquin

13. Finale from the 'Water Music'

Handel

14. Ecossaise in G

Beethoven

15. Fiddle Time rag

KB & DB

17
f
mf
21
mp
mp
25
29
mf
mf
33
cresc.
f
cresc.
f

16. Busy day

KB & DB

17. On the go!

KB & DB

18. Yodelling song

German folk tune

19. Takin' it easy: next page

20. Romani band

KB & DB

Nos. 19 and 20 are reversed to avoid a page turn.

19. Takin' it easy

KB & DB

21
mf
mp
cresc.
cresc.
26
poco rit.
a tempo
mp
p
31
4
36
mf
mp
41
pizz.
p
pizz.
p
dim.

21. Ten thousand miles away: page 28

22. I got those fiddle blues

KB & DB

No. 21 is shown on page 28 to avoid a page turn in No. 22.

23. Air in G

J. C. Bach

21. Ten thousand miles away

24. Prelude from 'Te Deum'

25. That's how it goes!

KB & DB

26. Hari coo coo

Indian lullaby

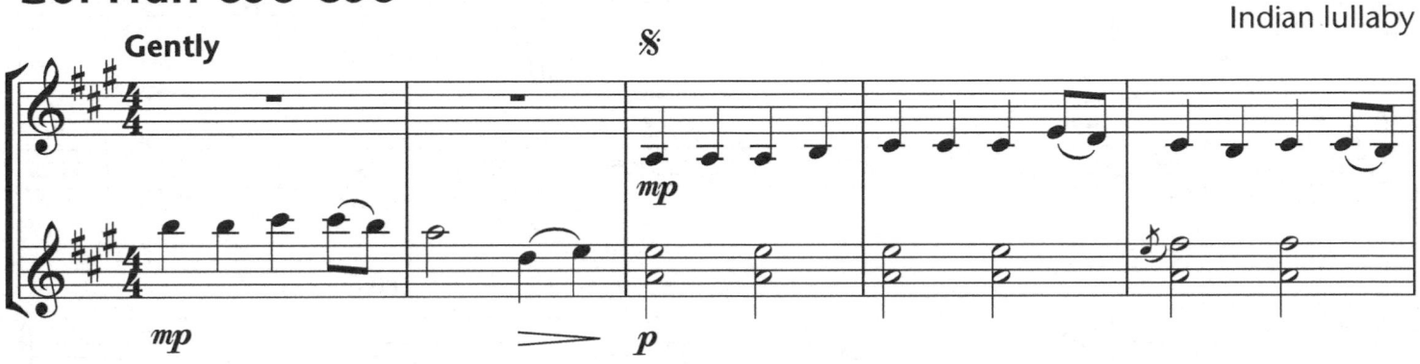

27. Summer evening

KB & DB

28. Flamenco dance

KB & DB

15
4
f
f
22
4
mp
mp
30
pizz.
f
f
38
arco
4
f
f
46
cresc.
ff
cresc.
ff

29. Adam in the garden

Jamaican folk tune

23
29
f
f
34
mp
mp
39
f
f

30. Somebody's knocking at your door

Spiritual

31. The old chariot

Sea shanty

32. Air

Handel

33. The wee cooper o' Fife

Scottish folk tune

34. Winter song

KB & DB

35. Rory O'More

36. Trick cyclist

KB & DB

37. Aerobics!

KB & DB

38. Caribbean sunshine

KB & DB